NOTEBOOK

This notebook belongs to

Thank you for purchasing one of our notebooks. We hope you are satisfied with your purchase, Please leave a review of your pad this will be appreciated massively.

Owthorne Notebooks

Made in the USA
Coppell, TX
15 February 2022

73640709R10069